Dedicated to Alex.

Never Tailgate on a Rainy Day

Tips and Advice for the New Driver

by Beth A. Schmidt

Dear New Driver,

Driving is a really important responsibility. It's bigger than cleaning your room, taking out the garbage, or being nice to your siblings. Being old enough to make choices that have significant consequences is a big deal. And you've got a lot to learn to be a good driver, to be safe for yourself and others.

It's a little scary. For you. And for the grown-ups who love you. Not because they don't trust you. Not because they think you can't be good at it. But because they are experienced drivers. They know things you haven't learned yet. And, more than anything, they want you to be safe and happy for a very, very, very, very, very long time.

This book includes some of the good advice I received as well as some lessons learned the hard way. I hope it helps you enjoy driving.

Motor safely.

BE PATIENT
WITH THE PERSON
TEACHING
YOU TO DRIVE.

He or she is probably terrified.

No permit needed.

Before you even start learning how to drive, sit in a parked car and learn to find the buttons for windshield wipers, turn signals, and the radio without looking at them.

1956 Ford Fairlane

When I went to take my driver's test . . .

I'd had a lot of practice and was very confident about passing. As
I started out, the officer told me to make a right turn, and I did.

He said, "Go on back to the parking lot. You're done."

I said, "Why?" and he told me that my tire had gone over the
yellow line as I made my turn. I was irate and sputtered,
"I know how to drive!"

"Maybe so, lady," he responded, "but you have to prove it to us.
We can't take your word for it."

—True story, from my Mom

Becoming a good driver.

Passing a driver's test doesn't make you a good driver; it just makes you a legal driver. Be aware that you have stuff to learn that only your own experiences will teach.

Pay attention. Be cautious. Then, when you're better at driving, pay attention and be cautious.

1960 Volvo

NEVER TAILGATE ON A RAINY DAY.

Don't tailgate on sunny days either.

"While driving and eating ice cream, in which hand should you hold the ice cream cone?"

Neither. You shouldn't be eating ice cream while you're driving!

— Advice from my Dad

1938 Studebaker Commander

1959 Chevrolet Impala

Stay in your lane.

When you first begin to drive, it takes a little while to get used to the perspective.

When in the driver seat, look out over the hood. From that angle, the center line of the hood represents where your right-side tires are.

In bad weather or darkness, when it's hard to see, you can get your bearings by following the tail lights of the car ahead of you. (Until they pull into their driveway.)

Remain calm.

Missing a turn or an exit on the highway is not the end of the world. You can always drive a bit farther and turn around or get directions to get back on track.

A spilled drink can be cleaned up. If a drink starts to fall or spill, let it go. Don't swerve or panic. You can clean the car later.

You may see odd and surprising things while driving. Control your shock. Stay focused on your driving.

1998 Camel

1955 Ford Fairlane

T PENNA T
67-171

"The only thing a blinking turn signal means is that it is working."

— Advice from my grandfather

Don't be a dipstick.

It's not enough to be a good driver.

You also need to be aware that there are a lot of stupid people in the world, and many of them have cars. They will do shocking, ridiculous, illegal, and dangerous things.

Expect the unexpected. And don't be one of the stupid people.

A note about swearing.

While swearing is generally frowned upon in polite society,
when you're driving, sometimes it's the better option.

Road rage (based in fear and caused by stupid people) can cause you
to lay on the horn, slam the brakes, speed up, or take your hand off
the wheel to gesture. These are not safe reactions. On the other hand,
swearing can be a perfectly safe way to vent fear and frustration.

You may come to realize that you are capable of incredible eloquence
in these situations. But it's important to remain aware of who is in
the car with you and whether or not your windows are open.

AS YOU GO FROM HERE TO THERE,

I HOPE
YOU FIND

BEAUTIFUL SURPRISES.

1968 Chevrolet Malibu

Backing into a fire hydrant while driving your parents' car is not the end of the world.

Tell your parents. They'll find out anyway.

Get an emergency roadside service.

It's good to learn when to pull over, when to go to a service center, and how to do some things yourself, like change a flat tire or check the oil. But, no matter how much more you learn, get yourself an emergency roadside service.

When you don't have a lot of money, it might seem unimportant to spend any on such a thing. But, even if you are only stranded somewhere one time in your entire life, it will be worth every penny.

You will get lost.

You will get lost while driving. You might get some bad directions or miss a turn. Signs might be missing. Your GPS might malfunction.

Or you could do something like drive to Akron when you were supposed to go to Columbus. (It happens.)

Don't panic. Find a place to stop and ask for help. Or find a place to pull over and call someone. Learn how to read a paper map.

Your sense of direction will get better as you get more driving experience. You will still get lost.

1936 Pontiac Sedan

ALWAYS KEEP A SPARE CAR KEY SOMEWHERE.

Other than inside the car.

Warning lights.

Anytime you're driving, it's good to know what the various dials and meters are showing you. Check the owner's manual for specifics, but be especially aware of these things:

- If the engine light comes on, pull over and call your parents or drive the car to a mechanic.

- If the brake light is on, check to see if you're driving with the parking brake on.

- If the gas gauge is on E, get the car to a gas station asap. Otherwise, you could end up having to coast backwards down a long windy hill, late at night, in the dark. And then have to walk up that long, dark hill all alone. And then you'll have to walk some more to find a friend and tell him the battery is dead. And then, when he gets his jumper cables and his car and comes with you and jumps the car for you and the car still won't start, you'll be laughed at for not having the sense to realize you had an empty gas tank.

HOW TO
USE A GAS PUMP.

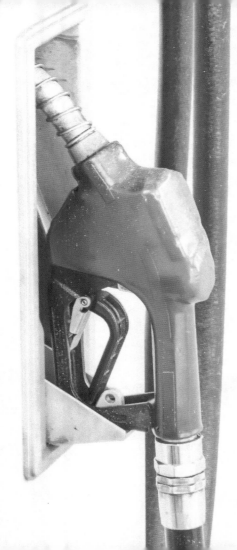

Know where the fuel tank door is, and pull up to the pump to position the fuel tank door on the same side as the pump.

Open the fuel tank door and remove the gas cap.

On the pump, insert credit or debit card as shown. (Or you can pay cash at the inside counter, but you usually have to pre-pay if using cash.)

Lift pump handle and push a button for the type of gas you want to buy. (Generally speaking, pick the least expensive option and don't get diesel unless you're driving a diesel vehicle.)

Fully insert the nozzle into the car; then, press and hold the trigger. Most pumps stop automatically when your tank is full. Otherwise, watch the meters on the pump and stop based on the number of gallons your tank holds or the amount of money you want to spend.

When done filling, replace the pump handle, reattach the gas cap (twist it to the right until you hear a clicking sound), and close the fuel tank door.

1959 Jeep (that is still in the family)

Get oil changes.

Get the oil changed on a regular basis. It's a basic and inexpensive way to help keep your car running well and avoid bigger, more costly problems.

Rule of thumb is every 3,000 miles.

But your car will not explode if you let it go a little longer than that.

Check your tire pressure.

Learn how to check your tire pressure and know where to go and how to add air when needed. Eyeball your tires every time you are walking to the car, and check the pressure monthly-ish. For an accurate reading, the tires should be cold (meaning the car has been sitting overnight or, at a minimum, for a few hours).

If you're not sure what pressure, use 32 psi. But the correct number for your vehicle will be marked on a label inside the driver's side door and/or in the owner's manual. (The number marked on tires is the maximum psi, not the recommended psi.)

Never drive on a flat. (Unless you are being chased by zombies.)

1974 Chevrolet Pickup

1947 Buick Special

HAVE AT LEAST ONE CAR
IN YOUR LIFETIME WORTH POSING WITH.

And always have a cool hairdo.

"I miss that car more than some people I've known."

My 1986 Mustang

THE WEIGHT
OF AN AVERAGE AMERICAN CAR IS
4000 POUNDS.

Not counting the pennies that will accumulate under your floor mats.

Always buy quality car wax.

- Wash the car well before waxing.

- Each time you wash the car, wax one section of it. That way, you never have to wax the entire car all at once.

- Never wax the car in direct, bright sunlight.

- You will wax your first new car more times than you will ever wax any other vehicles you ever own for the rest of your life—combined.

1953 Chevrolet Bel Air

1963 Ford Falcon and 1963 Ford Fury

LIFE IS
A LONG & WINDING ROADTRIP.
SEE THE SITES.
ENJOY THE JOURNEY.
TRAVEL WITH PEOPLE WHO LAUGH AT YOUR JOKES.

Be thoughtful about who you let drive your car.

1948 Dodge

A GENTLEMAN
OPENS THE CAR DOOR.

It's a secret way to say, "I like you."

Driving in real-life is nothing like driving in a video game.

- You can't beat someone up to get a better car.

- You can't outrun the police.

- There's no reset button.

- You'll see fewer hookers.

1963 Ford Falcon

Car ownership is expensive.

You may only think about the price of a car (which is a lot!), but there's more. There's insurance and gas and upkeep, like annual inspection, oil changes, and other things that will need to be replaced.

You might also want money to hire small children to wash your car for you.

When the time comes, buy a car you are able to afford without giving up the other things in life that make you happy.

There are people in the world who will judge you by what type of car you drive.

Anyone who does is a jerk.

The most important thing.

Don't take chances. If you have done anything that would make it unsafe or illegal for you to drive, don't drive.

Even if you think you'll get in trouble for whatever you've been doing. Even if you think your friends will make fun of you or be mad at you. Even if the cutest person in the world is involved. Do not get into a car if you (or the other person) should not be driving.

If you're somewhere and you need to leave and there's no safe ride, call a cab—or your parents.

Do the right thing. Make smart choices. And things really will turn out okay.

YOU ARE LOVED

MORE THAN WORDS CAN SAY.

Be safe.

share your driving stories,
tips for new drivers,
or favorite car photos:

facebook.com/nevertailgate
hello@bethaschmidt.com
www.bethaschmidt.com

6058622R00042

Made in the USA
Lexington, KY
11 February 2017